YOUNG PEOPLE'S STORY OF
OUR HERITAGE

YOUNG PEOPLE'S
STORY OF
OUR HERITAGE

THE AMERICAS

by

V. M. HILLYER and E. G. HUEY

New Edition Designed and Revised by Childrens Press, Chicago

Consultants

William T. Nichol, Principal
Charles Gates Dawes Elementary School, Evanston, Illinois

John R. Lee, Professor of Education
Northwestern University, Evanston, Illinois

Meredith Press, New York

*Illustrations
in the order
in which
they appear*

Library of Congress Catalog Card Number: 66-11332

Copyright© 1966 by Meredith Publishing Company. Originally published under the title of *A Child's Geography of the World* by V. M. Hillyer. Revised and Enlarged Edition, with new material by Edward G. Huey. Copyright, 1929, by The Century Co. Copyright, 1951, by Appleton-Century-Crofts, Inc. Copyright, 1957, by Mercantile Safe Deposit and Trust Co. All rights reserved. Printed in the U.S.A. Published simultaneously in Canada.

Contents

Acknowledgments

Cover drawing: Llama of Peru
John Hollis-Hollis Associates

Cover photograph: Mt. Eisenhower, Alberta, Canada
National Film Board of Canada

Page 2: Lake Louise, Alberta, Canada
Canadian Pacific Photo

Frontis: Orchids found in Brazil
Courtesy of Pan American Union

Opposite: Inca Chief near Cuzco, Peru
Courtesy of Pan American Union

_____

Designer: John Hollis

Project Editor: Joan Downing

Editorial Staff: Frances Dyra, Mary Reidy, Gerri Stoller

THE AMERICAS

Canada, Mexico, and South America

Introduction

In this book you will visit Canada, Mexico, Central America, and South America. You will see the beauty of the mountains, the mysteries of the jungles, the might of the rivers, the sweep of the plains. More important, you will see how people live and work and play.

A man who fishes from a kayak in an Arctic sea is much like the man who fishes from a canoe in a jungle river. It is the nature of the land and the resources of the land they live on that makes them live in different ways. A coffee grower on a South American mountainside and a wheat farmer on the plains of Canada have each learned to use the land they live on.

For many years, some of these countries themselves were mysteries. It took settlers in Canada two hundred years to find the fertile western plains. There are still unexplored jungles in South America.

Early explorers and map makers were always running into trouble. There were raging rivers and rugged, impassable mountains. There were endless tracts of wilderness and distances of thousands of miles. Most of these difficult problems of travel have been conquered by roads and bridges, trains and planes.

The wonder and beauty of the countries we travel through in this book remain, and we will see them and meet the people who call them home.

reading clockwise from above:

A drilling crew in Trinidad

A Peruvian girl

Farmers cultivating crops in Peru

Tuna fishermen off Hubbards, Nova Scotia

Mt. Tungurahua, a volcano in Ecuador

An Eskimo of the Northwest Territories, Canada

Bullfighting in Mexico

Instituto de Reforma Agraria y Colonizacion for World Bank

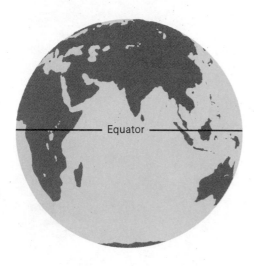

Eastern Hemisphere

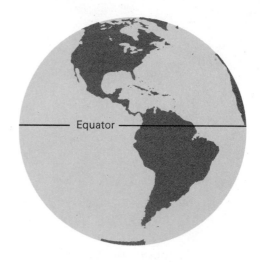

Western Hemisphere

Southern Hemisphere

Northern Hemisphere

The Surface of the Earth

The surface of the earth is divided into the eastern hemisphere and the western hemisphere. The continents of North America and South America are the western hemisphere. But each of these continents is also in another hemisphere, for the surface of the earth is also divided into the northern hemisphere and the southern hemisphere. The dividing line between these two hemispheres is the *equator* (ee-kway'tore). The equator is a line that goes all the way around the globe and is always exactly halfway between the North Pole and the South Pole. All the surface of the earth north of the equator is in the northern hemisphere and all the surface of the earth south of the equator is in the southern hemisphere. North America is north of the equator from Panama and South America is south of the equator from Panama.

The two continents look as if they had been pulled apart, stretching one continent toward the North Pole and one toward the South Pole. Panama seems to be a narrow thread connecting them. Canada, north of the United States, has part of its land inside the Arctic Circle. Cape Horn, in South America, is almost at the Antarctic Circle.

If you look at a map, you will see that the land of Mexico and Central America stretches to the east so that almost all of South America is not only south of North America, but also east.

A chain of mountains runs through western Canada, the United States, and south through Mexico, Central America, and South America. In some places these mountains are very high and in some places they are low. In some places they are very wide and in some places narrow. They follow the western edge of the continents. We have borrowed a word from the Spanish for such mountain systems. *Cordillera.* It means cord or rope.

The Cordillera in western Canada is four hundred miles wide. It includes the Rocky Mountains, or the Rockies, which end in Mexico between the Sierra Madre ranges. The South American Cordillera includes the mighty Andes.

above: The Cordillera

opposite: Maps of the hemispheres

National Film Board—Photo by Gar Lunney

Canada, the Friendly Giant

Canada is big. It is enormous. Only the U.S.S.R. is bigger. Canada, at its widest point, is almost six thousand miles across. In the north it reaches into the Arctic Circle.

If you looked down from a space ship over the North Pole, you would see something like the map that shows the United States, Canada, and the U.S.S.R. Look carefully at the map. See how Canada pushes up toward the North Pole, which is in the center of the picture. There are circles on the map marked 70°, 60°, and 50°. All of the land within the 70° circle has an arctic climate. It is very, very cold. It is a land of ice and snow. The sun does not rise above the horizon during the long, long winter. When the sun finally does get above the horizon it doesn't set for about a month.

The land within the 60° circle is subarctic, not quite so cold. The winters are about seven months long and the summers are pleasant.

The land within the 50° circle has a climate similar to that in the northern United States.

The southern border of Canada stretches for about four thousand miles along the northern border of the United States. Most of this border is only a line on a map. It has neither fence nor fort. Once the United States and Canada settled all arguments about the border, they agreed to live as friendly neighbors. This they have done for many years.

Most of the people of Canada live along this southern border—on a band of land about two hundred miles wide that lies along the United States.

The moderate climate is only one of the reasons for this. Almost half of Canada has a foundation of solid rock. This hard dome of rock rose millions of years ago. In many places it is bare. Those mountains of ice called glaciers have scraped their slow way over it. Dents in the rock surface have filled with water, making lakes. The weight of the glaciers pressed the dome of rock down in the north and water filled the hole to make the 500-mile-wide Hudson Bay.

This great layer of rock is called the *Canadian Shield*, or the *Laurentian Shield*. It covers almost half of Canada and has an area of about one and one-half million square miles. Much of the Canadian Shield is still wilderness. It is made up of rounded hills, many lakes, and swamps. Most of the land cannot be used for farming, but is rich in minerals. Much of the world's nickel, platinum, cobalt, uranium, gold, silver, copper, and iron are found here.

14

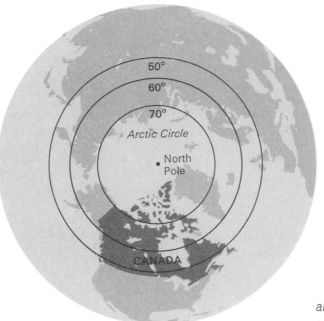

50°

60°

70°

Arctic Circle

• North
Pole

CANADA

above: The Northern Hemisphere

below: Copper mine, Quebec,
Canada

Early Explorers and Settlers

Two hundred years after Columbus found the New World, men were still looking for a short-cut to the spice islands. Champlain, a French map maker, went up the St. Lawrence River. Many other explorers came—French, English, and Scottish. They followed the rivers to Hudson Bay and they followed the rivers on the plains that drain into Lake Winnipeg. They found Great Slave Lake and Great Bear Lake in the north and followed the Mackenzie River to the Arctic Ocean.

None of the explorers found a short-cut. They found a great, broad land. They found people. There were Eskimos in the north and Woodland Indians in the east. Plains Indians hunted buffalo on the central plains. West Coast Indians went to sea in great canoes to hunt whales. They built totem poles to tell the story of their clan.

Most exciting to these early explorers were the furs they found instead of spices. Soon Indian canoes were traveling the waterways to bring furs to the trading posts. The main trading company, the Hudson's Bay Company, grew to be very powerful. At one time it claimed much of the land of northern Canada.

Settlers followed the fur traders. They came to make homes in a new land. Many Frenchmen settled on the fertile lowlands of the St. Lawrence River. They claimed the land and called the country "New France." Visitors today still find this part of Canada to be very much French in its customs, ideas, and traditions.

That was a long time ago. The English claimed this land, too, and there was trouble. At last an important battle was fought, before the time of the American Revolution. England beat the French and took over New France.

This was not the Canada we know today. For a long time there were scattered colonies that did not get along well together. Because of this, the country has been slow to develop. It was in 1867, almost a hundred years after the

American Revolution, that the colonies joined together to form the new Canada.

In the new Canada, the land was divided into provinces. There were four of them—Quebec, Ontario, Nova Scotia, and New Brunswick. In 1870 Manitoba became a part of new Canada. Now there were five provinces. British Columbia joined a year later. Prince Edward Island became a province in 1873 and there were seven provinces.

The provinces of Alberta and Saskatchewan were formed from some of the land of the Northwest Territories. The Yukon district became the Yukon Territory in 1898. Finally, Newfoundland became a province in 1949. Now Canada had ten provinces and two territories.

Canada was given independence from Great Britain in 1926, but remains a member of the British Commonwealth of Nations. Several countries belong to this Commonwealth, including Australia and New Zealand. These countries willingly joined the Commonwealth. This means they are independent and have their own government that makes the laws. The reigning monarch, the king or queen of England, is considered the head of the Commonwealth. Therefore the monarch is Queen of Canada as well as Queen of England.

Elizabeth II is now the queen. She was not elected queen by the people like the President of the United States is elected. When her father George VI died, Elizabeth became queen because she was the oldest child and had no brothers. When there are no boys in the royal family, the oldest girl becomes queen. Queen Elizabeth's oldest son is named Prince Charles. He will be the next king.

The countries belonging to the British Commonwealth expect to gain certain things. They have trade agreements that allow goods to go in and out of their countries. When goods go out of a country they are called exports. When they come into a country they are called imports. When a country imports or exports products, a certain amount of money is usually collected. This money is called a *tariff*. The members of the Commonwealth Nations do not have to pay this tariff on some of the products going in and out of their countries.

If any Commonwealth country feels she can get along better independently, she can leave the Commonwealth.

Early explorer in Canada with Indian guide

The Coastal Provinces

Nova Scotia, Prince Edward Island, and New Brunswick
If you approached Canada from the Atlantic, you would
come to the island of Newfoundland, Canada's newest
province. You would be on the great fishing waters called
the Grand Banks.

All continents have an *underwater shelf* around them.
The Grand Banks are on such a shelf. The water here is no
more than 100 feet deep. Beyond the shelf the bottom drops
away to the deep ocean floor, called the *abyss*. The earliest
explorers took home tales of the wonderful fishing on the
Grand Banks.

Fishing is still big business in Newfoundland. Cod and
salmon are plentiful along the shores and live lobsters are
packed and shipped to other countries. Thousands of small
boats go off and stay until they have caught as many fish as
they can carry. It is often foggy on the Grand Banks and
deep-throated foghorns can be heard as big ships from
Europe thread their way along.

The main industry in Newfoundland, however, is not
fishing but manufacturing. The most valuable product is
timber. It is used to make lumber, pulpwood, and news-
print. Mining is also very important to Newfoundland.
Copper, lead, silver, gold, and zinc are used for exports.

Boats go through a stretch of water called the Narrows
as they dock at St. John's, the capital and largest city of
Newfoundland. Signal Hill, above the harbor, is where
Marconi received the first wireless message sent across the
sea.

St. John's is a peaceful little city built on the hills.
Fishing fleets come and go from the port and much of the
catch is canned, frozen, dried, or smoked to be sold and
shipped away.

St. John's is quite a modern, bustling city, but away from
the city there are many old and picturesque fishing villages.

above: The Coastal Provinces

opposite: Canada

18

Arctic Ocean

ALASKA

Rocky Mountains

YUKON
TERRITORY

Great Bear Lake

NORTHWEST TERRITORIES

Mt. Logan

✱Whitehorse

*Mackenzie
River*

Great Slave Lake

*Rocky
Mountains*

Hudson Bay

*Laurentian
Mountains*

BRITISH
COLUMBIA

ALBERTA

CANADA

QUEBEC

NEWFOUNDLAND

Rocky Mountains

✱Edmonton

• Banff

MANITOBA

St. John's ✱

Vancouver
Island

Lake Winnipeg

*St. Lawrence
River*

NEW
BRUNSWICK

Grand Banks

✱Vancouver
Victoria

SASKATCHEWAN

ONTARIO

PRINCE
EDWARD
ISLAND

✱Regina

✱Winnipeg

Lake Nipigon

Quebec ✱

✱Fredericton

✱Halifax
NOVA SCOTIA

Lake Superior

• Montreal

*Bay
of Fundy*

Lake Huron

✱Ottawa

Lake Ontario

Toronto ✱

• Niagara Falls

*Lake
Michigan*

Lake Erie

UNITED STATES

Atlantic Ocean

Pacific Ocean

MEXICO

CENTRAL AMERICA

In Nova Scotia the capital, Halifax, is the chief winter Atlantic port for Canada. Tugs push ships from many countries into the harbor. An old stone fortress looks over the harbor. It was built many years ago by the British to keep invaders out of Canada.

Fishing is very popular in Nova Scotia. Cod, trout, swordfish, halibut, tuna, mackerel, herring, and salmon can be found swarming in the waters.

Many people from Scotland settled in a part of Nova Scotia called Cape Breton Island. In fact the Latin words *Nova Scotia* mean *New Scotland.* One very famous man from Scotland who visited here and built a summer home to enjoy the beauty of the island was Alexander Graham Bell. There is a museum on the island showing many of the different things that Dr. Bell worked on other than the telephone; they include airplanes, snorkels, iron lungs, and hydrofoil boats that can skim over the water at very high speeds.

In this village Baddeck—on Cape Breton Island many Scottish customs remain. Often you may see the people doing a dance called the Scottish reel or hear the sad music of the bagpipes.

Nova Scotia is famed for its beautiful shorelines and resorts along the coast. Yacht races are very popular. If you took a boat ride through this scenic country, you would see wooden lighthouses, towering fir trees, and toylike villages on the shores of Peggy's Cove.

Fishermen on the wharf in Bonavista, Newfoundland

Young girl does Scottish
dancing in Nova Scotia

National Film Board—Photo by Frank Royal

Along these shores the waters change twice a day. This change is known as the *tide*. The whole body of water moves slowly toward the land, or slowly away from it. Tides are caused by the moon and sun pulling water toward them.

The giant tides of the Bay of Fundy are spectacular. They are sometimes called the highest in the world. When the tides go out boats just sit on the dry harbor floor. One minute you may be swimming in the bay and the next there may be nothing but red mud to walk around in!

Miles of beaches and miles of farms make up Prince Edward Island. Most of the people farm the wonderful red soil of the island, or fish, or can the fish they have caught. The capital was first settled by the French as a trading post; later, when England gained control, it was named Charlottetown after Queen Charlotte, the wife of King George III.

The last of the Atlantic coastal provinces is New Brunswick. Although the winters are severe and heavy snow falls, the port of St. John on the Bay of Fundy is free of ice all year round. Here lumber comes from the forests in the province to be shipped to other parts of the world.

Mining and fishing are important in New Brunswick. Electric power is being used in factories. Most factories make things of wood from the forests.

The capital, Fredericton, is on the St. John River. This is wonderful hunting and fishing country. Along the river there are fields of hay and potatoes.

Quebec

An ocean-going ship can take you eight hundred miles up the St. Lawrence River to Montreal in the province of Quebec. Quebec is the largest Canadian province. The hard Canadian Shield spreads across most of it. There are many places in Quebec that look very much like France. It is here along the river that so many Frenchmen settled. Montreal has more French-speaking people than any other city in the world except Paris, France. There are French theaters, restaurants, newspapers, books, and shops. Montreal is the oldest and largest city in Canada. It was first visited by Cartier (car-tee-ay'), a French explorer, in 1535 and about seventy-five years later Champlain built a fort here. Gradually it was built into the city it is today. When the St. Lawrence is open and free from ice, large ocean liners and freighters dock at its port.

Mount Royal, on which stands Mount Royal Park, is an extinct volcano. From this park wonderful views of the city can be seen.

Cold winters, of course, bring ice and snow, and the people of Montreal skate, ski, and sled. One particular sport that involves expert skating is ice hockey. Two of the best hockey teams are in Canada—the Montreal Canadiens and the Toronto Maple Leafs—and nearly all the players on the United States' hockey teams come from Canada.

In 1967 Canada will hold an exposition, like a world's fair. It will be held on man-made islands in the St. Lawrence River at Montreal. This exposition will celebrate the one hundredth anniversary of Canada's Confederation, and will be called Expo 67.

Expo 67 will be a gigantic fair that will show man's achievements and hopes for the future. The nations of the world are going to participate. There will be a wonderland of exhibits showing science, exploration, modern living, the arts, and industry. The theme is "Man and his World."

At the exhibition there will be a modern community that shows the problems of every big city in the world. There will be pavilions of the nations and pavilions of all the

opposite: Ferry crossing the
St. Lawrence River at Quebec

right: Charming French
restaurant in Quebec

below: Canada vs. Czechoslovakia
in a hockey game

provinces of Canada. For entertainment there will be operas, ballets, symphonies, plays, singers, and dancers. If you get tired and want to take a boat ride you can do so in a water taxi, a Venetian gondola, a sampan, or a Mexican flower barge. It will be a wonderful sight to see.

Quebec City is divided into two sections called the Upper Town and the Lower Town. A huge medieval castle seems to frown down upon Quebec City, the capital of Quebec Province. This castle, Château Frontenac (shaa-toe frahn' tuh-nack), is now a hotel. Château Frontenac is in the Upper Town and its green roofs can be seen from many parts of the city.

In winter, Quebec becomes a snow-covered picture-post-card scene and horse-drawn sleds take passengers through the streets. Here again, as in Montreal, are interesting little streets and shops with French signs and restaurants and hotels that seem to belong in another world.

A glitter of ice crystals and snowflakes sets the scene for Quebec's famous Winter Carnival. You can see buildings and cars made out of ice, parades with people in bright costumes, snowmen made of fireworks, and dancers whirling in the squares. There are toboggan races, night skiers holding torches, and ice-canoe races over the ice-clogged St. Lawrence River. The winners of the race are considered heroes. A coronation is held to crown the lucky girl elected queen. The symbol of the Carnival is *Bonhomme Carnaval*, a living snowman. He can arrest you if you don't have the carnival spirit.

The Laurentian Mountains, with their many beautiful lakes, are in Quebec Province. There are many ski resorts in this area where there is always plenty of snow. This is also popular summer resort country.

Château Frontenac towers over the old section of Quebec City. Convenient winter transportation is the horse-drawn sleigh.

Ontario

The province of Ontario extends from the Great Lakes to Hudson Bay. She shares the Great Lakes with the United States. Other lakes in Ontario are the Lake of the Woods, and Lakes Nipigon, Seul, Nipissing, Simcoe, and Muskoka. Fishing in these lakes and hunting near them are exciting sports. Big black bears roam the forest.

The Canadian Shield is very poor farming country, but it has rich ore in it. Many mining towns are growing in Ontario where uranium, nickel, and other minerals are found. These little towns start with trailers in the wilderness but soon grow into modern communities with homes, schools, stores, office buildings, streets, and electricity. Sometimes after a town is built up the ore runs out. Then the people move to another area to work and a new town is built.

In the province of Ontario there are two things that we usually think come only from warmer climates—tobacco and grapes that are used for wine.

The largest city, and capital of Ontario, is Toronto. Toronto, like other large cities in Canada, is in the southern part of the country. From Lake Ontario you can see the skyline of Toronto reaching into the sky. Indians gave this place its name, which means "Place of Meeting." Perhaps this is one of the places on the Great Lakes where the Indians came with furs to meet the traders. This name is especially fitting now, for Toronto has become a very popular convention city.

Rainbow Bridge connects the United States with Canada over the Niagara Falls. The flags of the two nations fly on the bridge and a painted marker shows the boundary between the countries. The cities are named Niagara Falls, Ontario and Niagara Falls, New York. Because the falls are so powerful, great amounts of electrical power may be generated, or produced, from them. Canada and the United States share the power that is generated.

From Queen Victoria Park in Ontario you can see the beautiful Horseshoe Falls. Dressed in a slicker you can take a ride in the boat called the *Maid of the Mist* and ride

above: Ontario Province

opposite: The **Maid of the Mist** explores Niagara Falls

Tulips bloom on Parliament Hill,
Ottawa

The American Falls seen from Ontario, with Horseshoe Falls in
the background

below Horseshoe Falls. If you would rather not take the boat ride, you can have lunch in the Seagram Tower in Ontario and see the falls from the large windows. Many falls in the world are larger than Niagara, but the two countries have made Niagara Falls very exciting for visitors, with boat excursions and colored water displays at night. The falls are famous as a place for honeymooners.

The capital of Canada, the Federal District, is Ottawa in the province of Ontario. This attractive city has its government buildings on a hill called Parliament Hill which overlooks the Ottawa River. Unlike most capitals, this city was designed to be the capital city. It has broad streets and handsome buildings. In the spring, the city is filled with tulips.

During the last two weeks in May the Canadian Tulip Festival is held. Thousands and thousands of tulips bloom on the slopes, near the roads and streets, and in the gardens. Their beauty is spectacular.

In summer potted plants, bushes, and trees decorate Ottawa. Gothic-style government buildings surround a Peace Tower that has a clock at the top.

The national emblem of Canada is the maple leaf. In Ontario in the fall the maple leaves turn from green to red and gold in a blaze of color.

The northern part of Ontario borders on Hudson Bay. This great forest land is very cold and only about two months of the year are frost free. Deer and moose and fur-bearing animals provide game for hunters.

Places are often named after some city or river from where the settlers came. In Ontario there is a river called the Avon, and a city on that river called Stratford. In England there is a city on a river of the same name. That city is famous in England because William Shakespeare lived and wrote here.

Some years ago a Canadian thought that it would be a good idea to make Stratford in Canada like the one in England. Soon he had started a Shakespearean theater like the one in England. Many famous actors and actresses come every year to Stratford in Ontario to perform the plays of Shakespeare, and many visitors come to see them. So Stratford in Ontario is now famous in its own right.

Another famous place in Ontario is the home of Alexander Graham Bell. When Bell was a young boy he was very sick and his father moved to Brantford, Ontario for the good climate. It was here that he had the idea for the telephone. The house in which he lived is now famous and many people go to visit it each day. A Bell Memorial—a big stone sculpture of the inventor of the telephone—is near the center of the town. The very first long-distance telephone call was made from the Bell home to Mr. Bell in Paris, Ontario.

A Shakespearian actor in Stratford, Ontario

The Prairie Provinces

The wheatlands of Canada are the prairie provinces of Manitoba, Saskatchewan, and Alberta. They extend for miles between the Shield and the western mountains. Although wheat is grown here, forests and animals for hunting can be found too. Soil is fertile. But summers are short. The farmers have developed a kind of wheat that will grow in that climate.

Although Manitoba is considered a "prairie province," very little of it is treeless prairie. There are thick forests, and many rivers and lakes. The land is very rich and the deep fertile soil is the chief natural resource.

Because of the many rivers and lakes, Manitoba is very popular for fishing, boating, and swimming.

In Manitoba there is a famous garden. It is called the International Peace Garden. It is a symbol of the friendship between Canada and the United States. Half of the garden is in Manitoba and the other half is in North Dakota. Rocks from both countries show the International Boundary.

Winnipeg, the capital and largest city in Manitoba, is a famous cultural center. The Royal Winnipeg Ballet travels all through Canada and the Winnipeg Symphony Orchestra is very popular.

Saskatchewan is known for its wheat growing and petroleum refining. There are tall grain elevators all over the countryside. Saskatchewan is nicknamed "Canada's Breadbasket" because of all the wheat. Regina is the capital and largest city.

Aerial view of farm land in Manitoba, Canada

In the wheat fields it is not uncommon to see oil wells and drilling rigs. The main industry is now petroleum manufacturing.

When you enter the province of Alberta you might think you are entering the state of Texas. There are oil wells, ranches, wheat farms, and cowboys. They ride horses and hold rodeos just like those in the real West. Many parts of the province are very modern. There are skyscrapers, zoos, and big department stores.

Besides being western and modern, Alberta is also very beautiful. Winter sports are popular and many tourists go to a beautiful hotel called the Banff Springs Hotel. The view is breathtaking across the valley and lakes and mountains. There are aerial rides that can take you all the way up the side of Sulphur Mountain. Lake Louise, in Banff National Park, is one of the most famous lakes in the province. It is so blue and beautiful in its setting of snowy mountains that it can take your breath away when you look at it.

left: Banff Springs Hotel nestles in a mountain valley in Alberta

above: Mounties and Indians parade in Banff's Indian Days Celebration

There are also real Indians in Banff. For four days in July they have an Indian Days Celebration. Indians come from a nearby reservation and celebrate with rodeo events, races, ceremonial dances, and singing.

Alberta is very rich in oil. Some of the oil is buried in sand and engineers work very hard to find ways to get it out. One town called Edmonton has an area called "Refinery Row" because there is so much oil there.

One of the biggest companies in Canada is a railroad company called the Canadian Pacific. The railroad runs all the way across Canada from the Atlantic Ocean on the east coast, to British Columbia on the west coast. The Canadian Pacific owns all the hotels along the railroad. Along one part of the railroad you can see the dazzling scenery of Alberta—magnificent mountains and lakes.

35

British Columbia

The last of Canada's provinces is separated from the others by the Rocky Mountains. Because of the ocean currents, the coast of British Columbia is mild. But the interior can become very, very cold, especially in the mountains. Besides the Rocky Mountain chain, the Selkirk Mountains fill the center of British Columbia and the Coast Mountains come to the Pacific Ocean.

Off-shore islands make up part of the province. On one of these islands, called Vancouver Island, is Victoria, the capital of British Columbia. Victoria is a port and has ferry service to Vancouver, which is the largest city in British Columbia.

Victoria is warm and beautiful. The people are warm and friendly. There are gardens of lovely flowers all over the city and the cut flower industry is very important. When you walk along the quiet streets you see small English stores, horse drawn couches, and flower baskets swinging from lamp posts.

Vancouver is on the mainland. There are miles of beaches along the coast and plenty of trout for fishing. If you get tired of fishing, you can take a trip into the nearby mountains and hunt grizzly bears. Before the Canadian Pacific Railroad reached Vancouver, settlers had already come to British Columbia. Most of them came because of the Fraser River gold rush in 1858 and the Cariboo gold rush in 1862. The railroad did not reach the area until 1885.

Vancouver depends a lot on sea trade. Freighters, passenger liners, excursion boats, tugboats, fishing boats, and pleasure boats use the popular harbor.

Lakes are important in Vancouver. There is a famous fish here called the fighting Kamloops trout. He leaps high into the air and plops back into the lake.

opposite top: The city of Vancouver, British Columbia

opposite bottom: Spanish Banks Beach, a popular spot in Vancouver, British Columbia

National Film Board—Photo by Gar Lunney

The dusty main street of Barkerville, British Columbia

Vancouver is also cattle country. It is bigger than Texas. A famous ranch there called the Douglas Lake Ranch is so big that you can ride for two or three days on horseback and not get to the other side. It is the biggest ranch in Canada.

The scenery of Vancouver is spectacular. In summer roses seem to be everywhere. In winter ski lifts go up the magnificent mountains all the way from the city's edge.

The forests provide Vancouver with their leading industry. There are sawmills, pulp mills, and plywood plants. As in every large city, there are all kinds of people in Vancouver. The Chinese population is very large and Vancouver's Chinatown is one of the most picturesque and interesting places in the city.

The Yukon and the Northwest Territories

The Yukon Territory is north of British Columbia between Alaska and the Northwest Territories. Near the Alaska border is the highest mountain peak in Canada. Mt. Logan is 19,850 feet high. The summers are short in the Yukon and the winters are long and cold. In the northern part, inside the Arctic Circle, the sun shines for almost twenty-four hours during the summer and hardly at all during the winter. Fur trade, fishing, and mining are very important in the Yukon.

One Englishman who went to Canada to settle spent eight years in the Yukon Territory. He wrote about life and the men who went in search of gold in the Klondike in the Yukon. As you read his verse you can almost see the freezing, starving men who went to get rich and died instead. His name was Robert William Service.

Whitehorse is the capital of the Yukon Territory. It seems a small town when compared with many other capitals. Whitehorse is a distributing center for the furs and minerals found in the Yukon.

The Territory of the Yukon has a small population; there are only about ten thousand people. But in the past, when gold was discovered and men rushed to hunt for it, many people were living in the territory. You may reach the Yukon by car, for the Alaska Highway passes through the territory. During the short summer when the coast is free of ice, boats make the trip there. But the best way to reach this territory is by plane.

The Northwest Territories cover most of northern Canada—about one-third of the whole country of Canada. Much of the country in the Yukon and the Northwest Territories is within the Arctic Circle. In the very northern part of the Northwest Territories, land extends to within five hundred miles of the North Pole! Many islands and lakes dot this area. Much of the land is bare because it is too cold for anything useful to grow. For many years it was thought that hunting for fur-bearing animals would be the only way to earn a living in this northern land. Within the last sixty years, however, gold, oil, pitchblende, and ura-

above: An Eskimo woman plays with her grandson

---

opposite: Airport in the sparsely populated Northwest Territories

nium have been discovered and towns have grown up in the areas where discoveries have been made.

Many Eskimos, native to the cold regions of North America, live in the Northwest Territories. Hunting is their chief occupation. Eskimos were living in the cold regions when settlers first came. They lived on the ice itself or on the bare, cold, treeless plain called the *tundra*. Eskimos live in *igloos*, which is their name for a house. To build an igloo they take blocks of ice and fit them together. The blocks go round and round and get smaller as they reach the top. At the top there is a hole so air can get in. They fish for whales and walruses with a *harpoon*—a long spear with a barb on the end and a cord attached to it. The animal is speared and the Eskimo holds on to the rope while the animal struggles. To catch a large whale or walrus the Eskimos need skill and practice. Young boys learn from their fathers the proper way to harpoon.

Whales and walruses are used in many ways. Their oil is used for light and heat, their meat for food, and their skins, sinews, and bones for other things.

When Eskimos fish, they use boats like canoes. These boats are made with skins and are sealed so they are watertight. A small boat seating only one man is called a

kayak (kye'ack) and a larger one an *umiak* (oo'mee-ack).

The modern world has caught up with many of the Eskimos, but many of their customs and ways of life are still the same.

Maybe many things were never discovered in the north of Canada because it has always been so hard to reach. But today planes make runs up to outposts, towns, and villages. If someone gets sick and there is no one to help him in the village, a plane can come for the patient and fly him to a doctor or hospital. The Canadian Mounted Police do much of this work.

The Canadian Mounties came to Canada to answer the call of a wild frontier. During the 1800's white men were beginning to move into the vast "bush" of Canada. With him came problems. Cattle ranches were drowning out the Indian's buffalo grounds. Locomotives threw sparks into the dry prairie grass and started brush fires. The Indian was on the warpath. A British regiment was sent out to explore the problems. It was decided that a regular police organization would have to be formed. One hundred and fifty men were trained to maintain law and order along Canada's far-flung frontiers. These were the first of a police force that would be called the Northwest Mounted Police.

The Northwest Mounted Policeman quickly made a name for himself. His scarlet tunic and white helmet meant trouble for lawbreakers and help for their victims.

The Mountie is famous for always getting his man. This was difficult in the frozen north country. The Mountie was expected to bring his prisoner back in good health. This meant that the man had to be well fed and given regular exercise. Many Mounties have returned to headquarters in worse condition than their prisoners.

The Mountie tries to avoid using his gun. One Mountie tried to halt an escaping criminal by firing his gun in the air. When the criminal would not halt, the Mountie chased him for six miles. Although the Mountie was in full uniform and kit, he outran the fugitive and brought him back.

Regardless of the Mountie's bravery, he was never boastful. Messages sent back to camp by Mounties on the trail gave little hint of serious problems. If wolves were attacking nightly and the Mountie had to battle them off with torches, his message might have read, "Lost one dog." Details were left out. "Slight temperature drop" could have meant that the temperature was thirty degrees below zero and the Mountie was pushing against a blizzard.

Life has changed for the Mountie in many ways since he first came to Canada. Most Mounties now mount a car instead of a horse. Horses are still used in the "bush" regions; airplanes, boats, and trucks, however, are more common. Crime laboratories make the Mountie's detective work easier. Even the Mountie's name and uniform have changed. In 1903 the king changed the name Northwest Mounted Police to Royal Canadian Mounted Police. At this time, the small helmet was replaced by the wide brimmed stetson. This stetson and the scarlet uniform have become the symbol for one of the world's finest police forces.

Fifty years ago Canada lived off the land. The things that could be caught, grown, cut down, or mined made the economy of Canada. But Canada has changed. Now manufacturing is very important. Fish and animals are still caught, trees are still cut down, and wheat is still grown; but except for wheat, something must be done to most things before selling. Fish might be canned or dried. Trees are made into pulp and paper or other things. Animal skins are treated or even made into coats. The minerals are used in manufacturing too. Most of the factories where the manufacturing is done get their supply of electricity from water power. This power comes from the many waterfalls and from the fast flowing rivers. These are the things that make Canada a "rich country."

Mountie surveys the countryside in Alberta

Mexico, An Ancient and Modern Land

Look on the map at the Cordillera in Canada. Pick out that wide strand in the "cord" that is called the Rocky Mountains. If you follow this range south through the United States, it will lead you to a high plateau, or *tableland*, that is the *heartland* of Mexico.

Mexico City is on this plateau. Even though it is so far south, the climate is pleasant because the plateau is a mile high.

The plateau is not flat, for there are volcanoes on it. Some of them are still active.

Mountains called Sierra Madre (see-air'ah mah'dray) border the plateau on both sides. They join south of Mexico City and become one range.

Northwest Mexico is desert. Southeast Mexico is jungle. The low coastal plains and the valleys are hot.

At one time most Mexicans were farmers. They raised corn and beans as their main food. There are still many small farms in Mexico. But now oil is being shipped out of the country, and silver is mined. Industries are growing and roads are being built to join areas that are separated by mountains. Airplanes are used to reach remote areas of the country.

Mexico is the largest country in Middle America. Middle America includes Central America and the islands in the Caribbean. Middle America and South America were settled by Spaniards. We call them Latin-American countries.

Mexico City is the oldest city in the Americas. It was settled by the Aztec Indians hundreds of years ago. The Aztecs built their city over a lake with many small islands. This was not a primitive little city. It was a city of huge, well-constructed buildings. The Aztec Indians were a very civilized people. They knew how to build. They also knew how to farm and mine. They developed the lands around Mexico City long before the Spanish, under Cortes, ever saw Mexico. The Aztecs had a calendar and a written language. They had a good system of government, too.

CANADA

UNITED STATES

Atlantic Ocean

Sierra
Madre
Mountains

Gulf of Mexico

MEXICO

Pacific Ocean

Mexico City ✳ • Taxco
                    • Veracruz

• Acapulco

Yucatan Peninsula

Caribbean Sea

CENTRAL AMERICA

above: Modern skyscraper
in Mexico City

---

opposite top: Paseo de la
Reforma divides Mexico City

---

opposite bottom: Bullfighting
outside Mexico City

When Cortes saw their capital, he destroyed it. He then built a Spanish city on the same place. Even today Mexico City has some buildings that are like those Cortes built. But Cortes would not recognize most of the city.

Mexico City today is modern and beautiful. The Mexicans have long been leaders in the fields of modern art and architecture. The buildings in Mexico City are among the finest in the whole world.

The University of Mexico is an example of the best in modern architecture. The University was started in about 1550, but the modern buildings were not constructed until about 1950. Before they were begun, the Mexican government invited architects and artists from all over the world to make suggestions about how to build them. They wanted beautiful as well as useful buildings. The best suggestions were followed and the buildings are works of art.

One tall building, the library of the university, is almost completely covered with brilliant mosaics. It was designed by a great artist whose name is Juan O'Gorman. It is very colorful and beautiful. Many other buildings in Mexico City have mosaics, so the whole city is dotted with lovely artistic views.

Mexico City has touches of the whole world in it. You can learn a lot about Mexico in Mexico City, but not by just looking. It is so much like other great cities in the world that you might get confused about what is just Mexican alone. You would have the same trouble trying to understand the United States by seeing only New York City, or trying to get to know France by seeing only Paris.

Like Paris and New York and other big cities, Mexico City has a lot to do with other cities in the world. These other cities influence Mexico City, just as Mexico City influences them. And people come to Mexico City from all parts of the world. They come as tourists and also as businessmen.

In Mexico City, and in many other places in Mexico, you can find things that are Indian as well as Spanish. Remember, in Mexico—as in other parts of Latin America—the Indian has played an important part in developing the land. Indians were not confined to reservations in Mexico as they were in the United States. The Spaniards married Indians, and much of the population of Mexico is a mixture of both Spanish and Indian.

You know that the Aztec Indians settled Mexico City first, but they were not the only people who lived in the area in early times. Even before the Aztecs were in the land, another people had a civilization near Mexico City. We do not know very much about these people, but the pyramids they built are still standing in the region.

These pyramids are like the ones built in Egypt by the early Egyptians. We know that the people who built them and the other huge stone structures nearby had to be very intelligent. Remember, they did not have modern machinery to work with, but still they were able to build these amazing things.

The Mexicans have preserved the various Indian structures they have found. And they have preserved some of the early Spanish architecture as well. The famous silver city of Taxco (tass'ko) looks today much as it looked when the Spanish conquerors held it. In Taxco are some of the most important silver mines in Mexico. The Spanish wanted the silver almost as much as they wanted the gold that Mexico had. They wanted to send it back to Spain. They built Taxco to look very much as Spanish cities of the time looked. This look is called "colonial architecture," because it came to be when Mexico was a Spanish colony. In order to keep the colonial look in the city of Taxco, the people of that city have passed a law that says all new buildings must be built to look like the original colonial architecture.

Not only are there silver mines in Taxco, but there are also many fine craftsmen who work the silver. If you go to Taxco you can find many shops that sell the silver made by these craftsmen. They make bowls, cups, bracelets, rings and many other things of silver. Mexican silversmiths are famous throughout the whole world because their work is so beautiful.

Although Taxco was founded by Cortes, it was developed by a Frenchman named José de la Borda. He opened the mines in the eighteenth century—two hundred years ago. The buildings of the city are white with red tile roofs. The winding streets are paved with cobblestones. In the center of the city is a square with a little park and benches to sit on. All about the square are silver shops. At one end is an old church that de la Borda built in thanks for his good fortune. Like Mexico City, Taxco is in the heartland of Mexico. It is a pleasant and scenic trip by car or bus from Mexico City.

American Airlines

above: Children climb the Pyramid near Mexico City

48

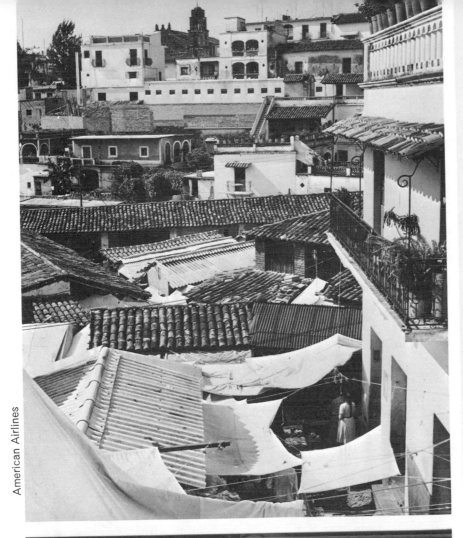

top left: Tile-covered houses in Taxco

top right: The central plaza, Taxco

bottom left: Santa Prisca Church, Taxco

bottom right: Happy Mexican children

Air France Photo

opposite: Mexican boy sits near a giant Olmec head
carved 1800 years ago

above: Moonlight in Acapulco, Mexico

There are two very important cities that are not in the
heartland but on the coasts. One is Acapulco and the other
is Veracruz.

Acapulco is on the Pacific coast in the humid, hot area of
Mexico. The map of Mexico will show you where it is. It is
one of the most famous vacation spots in the whole of the
New World. People come from all over the New World to
vacation in Acapulco.

Acapulco has many good beaches and all of the water
sports may be enjoyed here. Deep-sea fishing is, of course, a
favorite sport in Acapulco. A ride in a glass-bottomed boat
will give you a chance to see the beautiful marine life near
Acapulco. There are many modern and beautiful hotels. In
the mountains, not too far away, some vacationers even
hunt.

The other famous coastal city is Veracruz, which is on
the gulf on the east coast. It is also a favorite place for
vacationers, but that is not why it is so famous. It is the

largest commercial port in Mexico. From here goods leave Mexico—are exported—for all of the ports of the world. Other items come to Mexico from remote places by way of Veracruz. Much commercial fishing is also done in the Veracruz area.

For the tourist and for the student of early civilizations, there is no more interesting place in all the world than Yucatán. Here was once an even more highly developed civilization than that of the Aztec people. The civilization in Yucatán was developed by people called the Mayas. The people had big cities and pyramids with temples on top of them.

The Mayas had developed a class system with nobles, priests, and farmers. They had a system of laws, trade, religion, art, and writing. Their form of writing was *hieroglyphics*, or picture writing. They also knew much about mathematics and studied the stars.

Why did the Mayan Indians disappear as a civilized people? Why were they no longer important when Cortes first came to Mexico? The answers seem to be that they were a military people. After a while, the chiefs of the various Mayan cities began to make war on one another. They burned one another's cities and so destroyed themselves.

By the time Cortes came to Mexico as a conqueror, there was no great Mayan army to fight him. He had no trouble conquering these people who had once been lords of the land.

Now that you know about the Aztecs and the Mayas, you can see why the Mexican people are proud of their Indian background. But they have reason to be proud of that background for other reasons, too. Some of their greatest patriots have been Indian.

There were four groups of people who lived in Mexico during the Spanish era. There were the white Spaniards, the Creoles, the Indians, and the people of mixed Spanish and Indian blood, who were called *mestizos* (mess-tee′ zoz).

The Spanish had come as conquerors, and they made slaves of the Indians they found in Mexico. The Spaniards were very severe masters of the land.

Mexican Government Tourist Department

right: Aztec figures adorn the walls of the Temple at Quetzalcoatl

52

How Mexico Became Free

The fight for independence began in Mexico about 1810. This was a fight against the rule of Spain. The first leader of the Revolution in Mexico was a priest named Miguel Hidalgo. He and his Indian parishioners were defeated by the Spanish and by the Creoles who joined the Spanish in setting down the revolution. The Creoles were people who had pure Spanish blood, but who had been born in the New World. They were later to want a revolution, too. Why did they fight against Hidalgo? They did that because they wanted to rule over the Indians and the other people.

After Hidalgo was killed, another priest became the leader of the revolutionaries. His name was Morelos. He, too, was captured and shot. This happened in 1815, five years after the beginning of the revolution. The Spanish and Creoles continued to fight the revolutionaries, and finally were successful. But in 1820 a young Creole officer decided to turn the revolution into something that the Creole people wanted. This officer's name was Agustin De Iturbide (day ee-toor-bee' thay). He joined with the leader of the revolutionaries, and together they issued the Plan of Iguala. This plan was a declaration of independence. It was issued in February, 1821.

A year later, Iturbide made himself emperor of the land. The land then was much bigger than Mexico is now. It included New Spain and Central America, too. New Spain included Mexico, Texas, New Mexico, Arizona, California, some of Oregon, and some of the western part of Canada. Spain previously had claimed all that land, and now Iturbide claimed it from Spain.

Things did not go well for Iturbide. People revolted against him. They wanted liberty. One of the chief leaders of the revolts against Iturbide was an officer named Santa Anna. He began his revolt in Veracruz. Iturbide lost the fight and was shot.

Trouble began to come between the Mexicans and the people in the United States. Settlers from the United States moved into the northern land claimed by Mexico and there was a war over that. Santa Anna was the brilliant leader of the Mexicans. But he lost some important battles. Finally, the war ended when the United States bought New Mexico and California from the Mexican government for fifteen million dollars. Even before this time, Mexico had lost the part of Central America that it had claimed. Mexico had become the size it is today.

But the trouble was not over. The Mexican people were to have trouble with still another foreign government. This time it was with France.

Some of the people were trying to reform the government, which was still under the control of Santa Anna. Even though he had lost the territory to the north, he still was the leader. Finally, in 1855, these Mexican people got rid of him. Things were still not settled, however. Two sides were trying to get power. On one side were the Creoles and on the other side were the mestizos (of mixed Spanish and Indian blood) and the Indians.

The mestizos and the Indians had a great leader. He was an Indian, and one of the very poor people of Mexico. His name was Benito Juárez (beh-nee' toe wah' rez).

He was aided by the United States in his struggle for the liberty of all the people. In 1860 he was about to put new reforms into action, but then something happened. The United States became engaged in a civil war. The help that Juárez had been receiving from the United States stopped.

About this time, Napoleon III—who was the emperor of France—decided to take over Mexico. He sent Maximilian and his wife Carlotta to rule the Mexican people and he sent French troops to put down any rebellion that the Mexican people might start. Maximilian was an Austrian prince, but Napoleon made him Emperor of Mexico.

The Mexican people did not like to have France control their country. They had fought hard to free themselves from Spain, and now they were under the rule of France.

Maximilian was still emperor when the American Civil War ended. The United States now could help Juárez. Napoleon was having troubles in Europe and withdrew his French troops from Mexico. That was all the Mexican people needed. They captured Maximilian and finally shot him in 1867.

Juárez was once again in control. He began to reform the government again, but died before his reforms could be completed, and his enemies took over.

Many revolutions and reform movements followed in Mexico. They were like one big, very long revolution. It began in 1910 and didn't end until 1920.

This revolution was a conflict between the white population on the one side and the Indians and mestizos on the other side. The Indians and mestizos finally got the land reforms they wanted and the recognition they asked for.

Soldier who fought for Mexican Independence

Comision Federal de Electricidad, Mexico, for World Bank

Mexico was free and so were all of its people.

Today Mexico is a federal democratic republic. It is divided into twenty-nine states, the federal capital, which is Mexico City, and two territories. Each state has a capital.

After the end of the last revolution, Mexico began to make great progress both as a country and as a world power. Up until that time progress in the country had been very slow for many reasons. Many of Mexico's rulers had been much more interested in power for themselves than in improving the life of the people. And, of course, much time and money was spent during the many revolutions. For a long time most business was controlled by only a few people.

But today Mexico has become the leader of the Middle Americas. The nation is developing and making great progress in all areas—education, health, business, and culture. In some ways Mexico has been influenced by the United States, but never controlled by that country. Mexico is very independent.

Much business is done between the two countries because they are next-door to one another. One of the most important kinds of business that Mexico gets from the United States is tourism. Each year, thousands of people from the United States go to Mexico for vacations.

Todd Webb for World Bank

American Airlines

El Paso County Board of Development

American Airlines

reading clockwise from above:

Brilliant mosaics cover the library of the University of Mexico

Statues in the Cultural Museum in Juarez, Mexico

Busy Avenida Juarez, Mexico City

Hotels line the bay in Acapulco, Mexico

Mexican charros performing rope tricks

Sanalona Reservoir in the Sierra Madre Mountains, Mexico

Construction on the Santa Rosa Dam, Mexico

Mexican Government Tourist Department

American Airlines

Heavy earth-moving equipment used in highway construction, Guatemala

Central America

If you look on the map and follow the mountains of Mexico in the south, you will see that they curve toward the east. They run through the countries of Central America on a land bridge that joins the continent of North America to the continent of South America.

There are six independent countries on this curving stretch of land: Honduras, El Salvador, Nicaragua, Costa Rica, and Panama. British Honduras, the seventh country, is owned by Britain.

These countries were once a part of Mexico. You may wonder how seven separate countries came to make up Central America.

It was because of the land—the mountains, the rain forests, the volcanoes, and the canyons. People once lived in little pockets of settlement, for there were no roads or railroads. They were left in isolated groups and developed ways of their own. They became separate countries.

In Guatemala the Mayan Indians had a wonderful civilization fifteen hundred years before Columbus discovered America. The Indians in Guatemala are still a proud and independent people. They farm, weave, and make pottery. The capital of the country, Guatemala City, was completely destroyed by a volcano. It was rebuilt in 1916 as a beautiful, modern city. There are inland resort lakes in the country. Bananas are grown along the tropical, hot and humid coastal areas. The volcanic soil on the drier slopes of the mountains is good for growing coffee.

British Honduras originally was claimed by Spain, but no Spaniards settled there. When some British sailors found that the country was rich in mahogany trees, they moved in and went into the lumber business. The back country was impassable and the harbor was treacherous. The Spanish never took British Honduras and it still belongs to Great Britain. The capital city, Belize, is on the Caribbean. It has many canals running through it.

The independent country of Honduras is beautiful and rugged. From the rain forests the land falls toward the sea in a series of plateaus. The capital, Tegucigalpa (teh-goo-see-gal'pah), is on a plateau 3000 feet high. The country is rich in silver. When the Spanish were there they carried off a fortune in silver. The country has been independent since 1839. Gold and silver, fruit and cocoa are all important in the country today.

El Salvador is a small country south of Guatemala. It is on the Pacific side of the land bridge. The volcanoes in its mountains keep erupting. There are earthquakes, too. San Salvador, the capital city, was destroyed in 1917 by volcano and earthquake and was rebuilt as a modern city. The soil is very rich and coffee is the most important crop. Many people live in El Salvador. In spite of volcanoes and earthquakes it is a productive land, and no one needs to go hungry.

Nicaragua (nik-ah-rah' gwah) is one of the largest countries in Central America, but it is sparsely settled. The country is rich in gold, silver, and mahogany. There are coffee plantations, and bananas grow well. The country has developed slowly, however, because the government was not stable. There were nearly 400 dictators over a period of sixteen years. A dictator rules alone and has absolute power. Many dictators do not use their power well and are often more interested in gaining wealth and power for themselves than they are in the welfare of the people. In Nicaragua, with so many rulers in such a short time, it was very difficult for any of them to accomplish much.

Cotton and coffee have become important exports in the last ten years. The low coastal land along the Caribbean is

opposite top: Workmen build sheds at the Port of Corinto, Nicaragua

opposite middle: Costa Rican girl working in a candy factory

opposite bottom: Young boy learns carpentry in Guatemala City, Guatemala

TAMS of Panama Inc. for World Bank

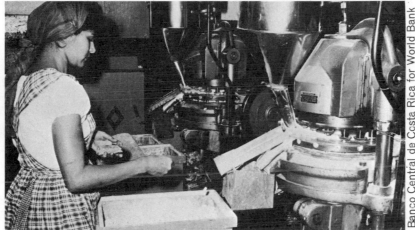

Banco Central de Costa Rica for World Bank

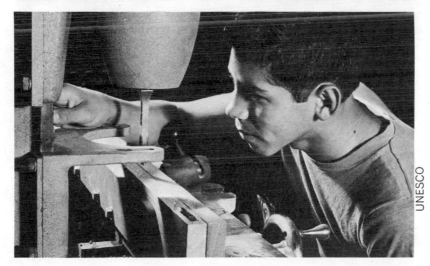

UNESCO

flat and wet. It rises to a plateau broken by mountains. Most of the cities are on the Pacific Ocean in the region of plains and lakes. The capital, Managua (mah-nah'gwah), is here. This is the port through which the trade of the country flows. Someone once wrote a popular song about Managua, Nicaragua. It is a very musical name.

Costa Rica (koss' tah ree' kah) is a small country between Nicaragua and Panama. It has a long coast along

the Pacific and a shorter one along the Caribbean. The Caribbean coast is swampy jungle. The four main cities, half the population, and most of the coffee plantations are in the central highlands. There are four volcanic mountains in the highlands and two of them are active. The Pacific lowlands are hot and wet, like those on the Caribbean, but they become dry enough in the northwest for cattle raising and farming. The University of Costa Rica is run by the government. The government spends more money on education than on anything else, so most of the people can read and write. The land bridge of Central America grows narrow at Costa Rica. From one mountaintop you can see both the Atlantic and the Pacific.

The country of Panama is a republic. It is a narrow neck of land between Costa Rica and Colombia, South America. There are several mountain ranges in Panama and hundreds of rivers. Most of the country is covered by thick jungles in which there are a few patches of prairie.

---

opposite: Aerial view of Cristobal in the Panama Canal Zone

Panama once belonged to Colombia. But when Colombia refused to allow the United States to build a canal across the *isthmus*, the narrowest part of the land, Panama was encouraged to revolt. It became independent in 1903.

In Panama, the Pacific Ocean is only a few miles from the Atlantic Ocean. But to get from one ocean to the other, ships had to go 10,000 miles around South America! A canal through the isthmus seemed a very good idea. The French had tried to build one and failed. The United States spent ten years building the present canal. They chose a fifty-one mile course between the mountains. Even so, locks had to be built to lift the boats 285 feet over the center of the isthmus.

Panama is a crossroads for world shipping. It is also a crossroads for air travel between North and South America. The north and south sections of the Inter-American Highway meet at the canal. Someday you will be able to drive from Alaska all the way through South America!

---

opposite: Miraflores canal locks in the Panama Canal

Courtesy of Pan American Union

Contestant in the Calgary Stampede,
the Annual Rodeo in
Alberta, Canada

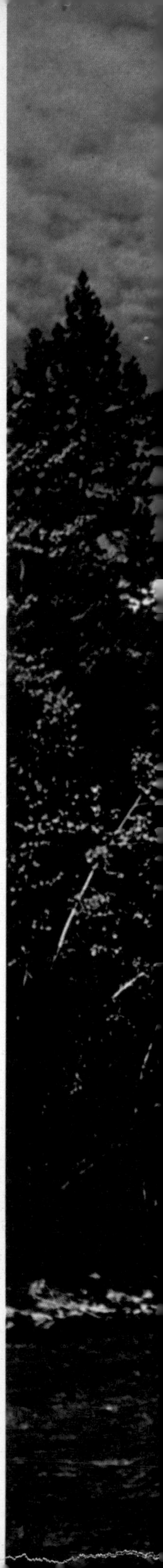

––––––––––––––––

Mt. Robson, one of the many
mountain peaks in British
Columbia, Canada

Bob Brunton—Hollis Associates

66

City lights reflected in the St. Lawrence
Seaway brighten the night view of
Montreal, Canada

The rocky Newfoundland coast near wonderful
fishing waters of the Atlantic Ocean

A cart pulls sisal,
a plant used in
making rope, in Mexico

This market
in Yucatan is typical
of markets
in Latin America

Acapulco Bay, Mexico, is a
natural vacation paradise

above: Calypso singers delight both the natives and visitors
in the West Indies

right: Bathsheba coast on the Atlantic Ocean side of Barbados

Palm trees line
Copacabana Beach
in Rio de Janeiro,
Brazil

Photo by Chan Forman

Pan American Airways

Flame trees brighten the landscape in Venezuela

The ancient Inca city of Cuzco, Peru

The fierce jaguar is hunted in the hills surrounding Acapulco

Rich vegetation covers
much of Argentina

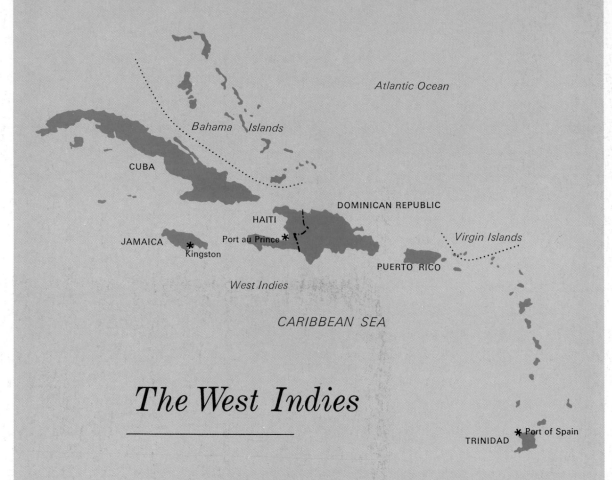

Atlantic Ocean

Bahama Islands

CUBA

DOMINICAN REPUBLIC

HAITI

Port au Prince ✱

JAMAICA
✱
Kingston

Virgin Islands

PUERTO RICO

West Indies

CARIBBEAN SEA

The West Indies

✱ Port of Spain
TRINIDAD

You might think that any place called the "Indies" would be near India, but the West Indies is a long, long way from India—in the western hemisphere. They are part of Middle America. How did these islands in the Caribbean ever come to be called by the name "Indies"?

There are some other islands that are in the east, on the other side of the world from the Americas. These islands are called the East Indies. People in Europe had discovered that these islands produced a lot of things they wanted, such as spices. They traded with these islands for a long time, and they do today. When people still thought that the world was flat, they believed that the only way they could get to the East Indies was by sailing east.

Columbus thought that the world was round, so he decided to reach the East Indies by sailing west. He sailed and he sailed and finally he found islands. He thought the islands were the East Indies. Really they were what we now call the West Indies.

Columbus had found a new land, although he did not know it at the time. He found men living on the islands.

They were strange looking to Columbus and his men, because they painted their faces and wore feathers in their hair. Columbus called these people Indians. Later, other people called the painted men *Caribs* which means "brave." The sea around the islands came to be called the "Caribbean Sea" after the Caribs.

Later explorers discovered that there was much gold and silver in this new land. They discovered this because many of the Indians they saw wore gold and silver ornaments.

A basket vendor in Haiti

The Indians had found the gold and silver in the ground and had learned how to work it.

The Europeans stole the gold and silver from the Indians and then they stole their land, too. They started settlements mostly so they could get the gold and silver and send it back to Europe. Most of the conquerors of the Middle Americas and South America were Spanish. Their kings were very powerful. One of them, Philip II, wanted to conquer the whole world. For this, of course, he would need a lot of money. So the Spaniards went to work. They took more and more riches from the New World to send to the Old World —especially to Spain.

All of these riches were sent by ship. It was not too long before sea robbers, or pirates, began to capture the ships so that they could have the riches for themselves. Some of the pirates robbed for themselves, but some of them, especially in the days of Philip II, were English adventurers who captured the Spanish ships so that they could take the riches back to England. Why did they do this?

They did it because Philip II was planning to conquer England at the time. He needed money to build a big fleet, and much of his money came from the riches of the New World. The English decided that if they could keep these riches from getting to Spain, they could stop Philip. Philip complained about the pirates to Queen Elizabeth I, who was then the ruler of England. She pretended to be angry with the Englishmen who pirated Spanish ships, but she never punished them.

You can see that piracy played a big part in the history of the world. It was never a respectable business, of course, and many pirates who were caught were hanged.

The pirates did their business from the islands in the West Indies, because these islands have many coves where ships can hide. Most of the islands have high hills, too, for from them the pirates could see ships that were returning to Europe with riches. After they had spotted the treasure-laden ships, they could rush to their own ships and chase after them.

There are no more pirates, but many ships from all over the world still carry riches from the New World over the Caribbean Sea. Most of the modern riches are things that the pirates would not have been interested in. They include sugar cane, tropical fruit, petroleum, tobacco, coffee, and cocoa. Some gold and silver is also shipped, but mostly in the form of ornaments. These riches come from all of the Latin American countries and from the West Indies, too.

The people who live in the West Indies sell a lot of these products themselves. But they have another very important industry. It is tourism.

The islands in the Caribbean are very beautiful and they have been developed to make them attractive to vacationers. It is easy to get to them, too. Not only ships but also airplanes arrive at many of these islands daily. Tourists bring a lot of money to the West Indies and many of them have become resort islands.

There are only four independent countries in the West Indies. They are Cuba, Puerto Rico, Haiti, and the Dominican Republic. All of the rest of the islands are possessions of other, large countries. Puerto Rico is a *commonwealth* of the United States, although it is an independent country. The United States owns three of the Virgin Islands, which are very near Puerto Rico. These Virgin Islands are *possessions* of the United States.

England owns the islands of the Bahamas and some other small islands. The biggest English island is Jamaica. Its capital is Kingston. This city was begun in 1692, after the former capital, Port Royal, slid into the sea with all its houses, palaces, and people.

Jamaica is one of the islands of a group called the Greater Antilles. Cuba also belongs to this group and so do the islands of Hispaniola and Puerto Rico. The capital of Cuba is Havana. Cuba is a land of sugar cane and fine cigars. But it is a land much upset in recent years by troubled politics.

Haiti and the Dominican Republic are located on the island of Hispaniola. The capital of Haiti is Port-au-Prince and the capital of the Dominican Republic is Santa Domingo. The Dominican Republic is another land that today is suffering because of the political situation.

Columbus was buried in Haiti. Later, his bones were moved to Spain where they were buried in a great cathedral. Some people say that it was not actually the bones of Columbus that were taken to Spain, but the bones of someone else. No one can really be sure of that.

British Overseas Airways Corporation

reading clockwise from right:

Donkey carts haul cane sugar to
the factories, Barbados

Fishnets dry in the sun
in Georgetown,
Bermuda

Cattle doze
under the trees in
Jamaica, West Indies

Tower Isle Beach in Jamaica

Boats used for work in Barbados

British Overseas Airways Corporation

British West Indian Airlines

American Airlines

British Overseas Airways Corporation

The Continent of South America

On a map the continent of South America looks like a triangle, drifting toward Africa. It is held securely to Central America by that mountainous Isthmus of Panama.

The mountains of Panama meet the mountains of South America. There is that Cordillera again. The Andes Mountains extend 4,500 miles along the western coast of South America. They reach a height of 22,000 feet.

These mighty mountains may hold South America together, but they also divide it. They are much more difficult to cross than the Rockies in North America.

For many years, the three countries on the Pacific coast of South America were cut off from others on the continent. But today airplanes make regular flights and bring the areas within minutes of each other.

Two great river basins cut through the central plain of South America. The Amazon rises in the Andes and flows across the continent to the Atlantic Ocean. The Paraná River flows south through the center of the plain and also empties in the Atlantic.

The eastern bulge of the South American triangle is high mountainous plateau that slopes inland toward the plain.

South America has every kind of climate. There are snow-capped mountains and dense, unexplored rain forests. Grasslands cover much of Argentina. The cold, desolate southern tip of the continent reaches toward the antarctic regions.

Colombia is the country you enter if you come to South America from Panama. This is the only South American country that touches both the Atlantic Ocean and the Pacific Ocean. Colombia is a tropical country with the Andes running through it. Most of the people live in the western part of the country. They live in the two river valleys that run between the mountain ranges. There are many coffee plantations on the slopes of the mountains. The eastern part of the country runs off into plains and unexplored jungles. The inland capital, Bogotá, once could be

Caracas ✳
Lake Maracaibo
TRINIDAD
VENEZUELA
Orinoco River
BRITISH GUIANA
Georgetown
✳
DUTCH
GUIANA
✳ Paramaribo
✳ Cayenne
FRENCH GUIANA
Andes Mountains
✳ Bogotá
COLOMBIA
✳ Quito
EQUADOR
Guayaquil •
Iquitos •
*Amazon
River*
Manaus •
*Amazon
River*
• Belem
PERU
Lima
✳
Machu
Picchu ✳
Cuzco •
Lake Titicaca
✳ La Paz
BOLIVIA
*Andes
Mountains*
BRAZIL
✳
Brasilia
PARAGUAY
Pacific Ocean
✳ Asuncion
*Paraná
River*
• Rio de Janeiro
ARGENTINA
URUGUAY
Valparaiso •
✳
Santiago
Buenos Aires ✳
✳ Montevideo
Plata River
CHILE
*Andes
Mountains*
SOUTH AMERICA
*Strait of
Magellan*
Tierra del Fuego
Cape Horn

reached only by a difficult journey. Now airplanes, travel there easily. Bogotá is a modern city with many very old Spanish buildings. There are several universities in the city.

Venezuela is next to Colombia. When explorers first came to the northern shore of South America, they found Indians living in houses built on stakes in the water. This reminded them of a city of canals in Italy called Venice. So they named this new land "Little Venice," which in Spanish is Venezuela. The 1600 mile long Orinoco River has seventy mouths. They form a huge *delta*, or deposit of clay and mud in the shape of a triangle. There are about a thousand other rivers in Venezuela. Small wonder that the Indians built their homes on stilts! Lake Maricaibo (maar-ah-kye′bo) lets ocean vessels sail inland for 130 miles. The lake is dotted with oil derricks. It is hot and humid in this area. South of the Orinoco there are uninhabited plains and unexplored jungle. Most of the people live in an area that is only about one quarter of the country—the Andes highlands near Colombia. The capital, Caracas, is on a high plateau. Not long ago, about half the people lived in shacks with mud floors and walls. The government now is working

opposite top: Storage reservoir near Bogotá

opposite bottom: Crew working on a railroad bridge

left: A new highway system in Venezuela

to build better homes. Farming, which used to be the main occupation in Venezuela, is now less important to the country than the production of oil.

Off the shore of Venezuela is the island of Trinidad. It is mountainous and tropical. There is a strange lake on this island called Pitch Lake. It is filled with a kind of tar called *asphalt* instead of being filled with water. The asphalt is dug up, loaded onto ships, and sent to other countries to be used to make roads. A strange thing about this lake is that its level does not go down much. As asphalt is taken from it, more seems to flow in to fill it.

South of Venezuela on the Atlantic there are three little countries that are really colonies of foreign countries—the only ones in South America.

British Guiana is almost all jungle. Way back in the wilds of the country there is a waterfall nearly five times as high as Niagara. Not many people see it, because it is so hard to reach.

French Guiana, rich in gold, iron, lumber, and chicle— used in chewing gum—had a grim past. The dreadful French prison colony of Devil's Island was here.

Surinam lies between the two Guianas. It was once called Dutch Guiana. It still belongs to the Netherlands. It is rich in bauxite, from which aluminum is made.

Brazil sprawls across the whole, huge bulge of the triangle of South America. There are many good ports along the Atlantic Ocean. The upper half of the country is dominated by the Amazon River and its many branches. This mighty river gets so broad that you cannot see across it. It empties more water into the ocean than any other river in the world. All the great rivers in South America flow to the Atlantic. The Amazon is an important and necessary transportation link for many trading communities in Brazil.

Brazil is bigger than the United States. It gets its name from the brazil tree that is used for making dye. It would have been more fitting if the country had been named "Rubber" or "Coffee." Rubber and coffee are more important to Brazil than the brazil trees.

The land around the Amazon River is called *selvas*, which means "woods." It is not only woods, but jungles and swamps—wild, hot, unhealthy country. It is so hot and damp that everything grows big and thick and fast. Water lilies have leaves as big as the top of a dining room table. It is hard for a man to make his way through the tangle of

opposite: Aerial view of a highway being built in Venezuela

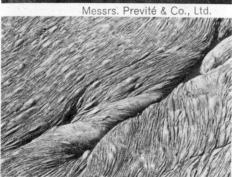

Messrs. Previté & Co., Ltd.

above, left top: Barrels
of asphalt, Trinidad

above, left bottom: The
surface of Pitch Lake

above right: Amazon fisherman

right: Amazon boat train

growth in the jungle. This jungle growth comes up again almost as fast as it is cleared.

Many animals live in the selvas, but few men. Most of the men who do live here are Indians. There are monkeys and parrots. There are butterflies and moths of great size and beautiful colors. Huge snakes called *boa constrictors* hang from branches, looking like heavy vines. Animals that are fooled by this are caught by the huge snake, who coils around them and hugs them to death. Also in the selvas are lazy, sleepy animals called sloths that hang by their toes from the trees.

There are animals like dragons, called *iguanas* and huge bullfrogs whose croaking sounds like the roar of lions. Another snake like the boa constrictor that the natives really fear is the *anaconda*. This snake is not really very

above left: Alligator

below left: White-faced monkeys

above right: Coiled anaconda

dangerous, but it grows to be very large, sometimes thirty feet long, and it kills its prey the same way the boa constrictor does. The anaconda has no venom and cannot poison a victim, but it is so powerful it does not need poison. Alligators and crocodiles can be seen as you travel down the river. Sometimes the crocodiles go ashore and eat the cattle and dogs that belong to the Indians.

The noises of the jungle are not like city noises. Along with the bullfrogs' croaking can be heard the howling of the monkeys, the screaming of the hawks and eagles, the twittering of many birds, and the rustling of leaves as animals and insects move around unseen in the growth.

You may wonder why anyone goes to the selvas at all. They go hunting for animals for museums and zoos, but the chief thing they go hunting for is the juice or sap of a tree that grows wild in the selvas. Much of the land in the heart of the jungle is still unexplored but in the explored land man can find rubber.

Settlers found the Amazon Indians playing with bouncing balls. They had seen nothing of the sort before. These balls, they found out, were made of the sap of a tree. Then they found that lumps of it would rub out writing—so they called it rubber. They also found that they could make automobile tires, stretch bands, and boots of it. Soft rubber and hard rubber and pully rubber and springy rubber are all made from the sap of the rubber tree by treating it in different ways.

Men go through the selvas and wherever they find a rubber tree they cut notches in its trunk and fasten a cup underneath to catch the tree's sap. Then they go around again and empty the cups of rubber sap into a bucket and carry the bucket to their camp. When they have collected enough sap, they take a stick, pour some of the sap on it, and dry it over a fire. They do the same thing again and again until there is a big lump of rubber on the stick. They pile these lumps of rubber into canoes and go down the Amazon River to larger boats that take the rubber to other countries. The first rubber was found along the Amazon.

---

opposite: Man collects sap from tapped rubber tree in Brazil

A city almost a thousand miles up the Amazon River from the Atlantic port of Belem is Manaus. Early in the twentieth century there was an enormous market for the rubber found in the jungle. Many settlers came to Manaus and worked the rubber industry. Some beautiful buildings were built and many people became very rich. Many of the buildings now stand as a reminder of this past, in particular a superb opera house. For about ten years, singers from many parts of the world ignored the possibility of danger and disease and came to perform in this opera house. The money they earned performing here was much more than they could earn in other places. After rubber plantations sprang up in Asia, much of the business around Manaus stopped. Now it is a glorious town in the middle of the jungle, with very few people living in it. It is like a ghost town.

There is something that grows in Brazil that is now more important than rubber. It is coffee. Coffee doesn't grow wild in Brazil as the rubber tree does. In fact, coffee didn't grow in Brazil at all until some men brought coffee bushes from across the ocean and planted them there. They planted them on high ground near the shore—not in the selvas. They found that the high ground and the weather were just exactly right for growing coffee, and now much more coffee grows in Brazil than in the place where coffee came from first. Indeed, more coffee grows here than in any other place in the world.

Coffee grows on a small tree, and the coffee berries look something like cherries. Inside each cherry-like berry are two seeds. These seeds are what we call coffee beans. But before coffee can be made into a drink the coffee beans must be toasted brown and then ground.

---

opposite: Heavily fruited coffee tree in Brazil

Courtesy of Pan American Union

One New Year's Day a long time ago a man was sailing along the coast of Brazil when he came to what seemed to be the mouth of a river. Since it was the first day of January he named the place River of January, which in his language, Portuguese, was Rio de Janeiro (ree'o day zhah-nair' o). His river turned out to be only a harbor, but the city that grew up there is still called Rio de Janeiro. In the harbor of Rio, as it is called for short, there is a huge rock called Sugarloaf Mountain. As you see Rio from a ship, the low mountains behind the city look like a "Sleeping Giant," and that is what they are called.

If you fly over Rio you really get a complete view of the city. Along the curving harbor is a beach with sparkling white sand and a wide avenue. You can see that the harbor is sheltered and many boats are anchored there. All along the broad avenue are large steel, concrete, and glass buildings. If you come overland, you will first fly over a high hill with a large statue of Christ and then see the city spread out below you. If you don't fly to Rio, you can take a trip up to the mountain on a railway and get a view of Rio that shows how it is squeezed between the ocean and the mountains.

Much of Rio is very beautiful, but much of it is not beautiful at all. It is a city with many well-educated people and many who are uneducated, many very wealthy people and many who are very poor.

Probably the most exciting time to see Rio is at carnival time. Carnival is held before the season of Lent. People dance in the street, bands play, costumed people parade, and huge banners are carried for days of celebration. For weeks before the carnival begins people frantically make preparations and the streets buzz with activity. On the

Panoramic view of the harbor of Rio de Janeiro

Sunday before Ash Wednesday everything seems to explode and the carnival begins. From that time until Ash Wednesday some people do not sleep at all, but dance and sing and parade through the streets.

On the top of Sugarloaf Mountain is a radio station. You can take a trip here in a car like a bus that goes through the air—an aerial cable car. Again you can see the beautiful Copacabana Beach spread below you and maybe get a few shivers at being so high in the air in such a little car!

Rio de Janeiro was once the capital of Brazil, but now the new inland city of Brasilia is the capital. The first government employees moved into this city in 1960. Brasilia is built on the high plains six hundred miles northwest of Rio. The earth seems to be red and the buildings are some of the most daring modern buildings in the world. The city has everything that any city needs.

You remember we mentioned that the name meaning River of January is not a Spanish word. Usually we think of the South American countries as having Spanish beginnings. This is not the case with Brazil. Brazil was settled by people from Portugal, and it was ruled by Portugal for about three hundred and fifty years before the Brazilians gained their independence. That is why Portuguese is the language of Brazil.

More coffee is shipped from Rio than from any other place in the world except another place on the coast of Brazil just south of Rio. This other place is called Santos. Santos, too, has fine beaches and modern buildings and miles of docks. Some of the coffee is roasted and ground before it is shipped. Men are employed to taste the coffee to be sure that it is good enough to ship.

opposite top: Cable car transports visitors to Sugar Loaf Mountain

opposite bottom: Gigantic statue of Christ overlooks Rio

Courtesy of Pan American Union

above: A gaucho in his colorful costume

opposite top: An Andean village in Uspallata, Argentina

opposite bottom: Cattle round-up on the Argentina pampas

When the Spaniards came to South America, to the land south of Brazil, they saw Indians there wearing silver bracelets and silver necklaces. They supposed there must be much silver in the land, so they named the country "Silver Land," which in their language is Argentina. Argentina, as it turned out, really had very little silver, but we call it Silver Land just the same.

Although Argentina has little silver, the people there have quite a lot of money. They do not get the money out of the ground from silver mines. They make it by selling wheat and meat. It would have been more fitting if they had called Argentina "Wheat Land" or "Meat Land" instead of "Silver Land," but not nearly so pretty. In Argentina there are enormous farms that produce wheat and corn. There are also enormous fields called *pampas* where cattle and sheep are raised. The men who look after these cattle and sheep are called "*gauchos*." Gauchos wear *ponchos*. A poncho is a kind of square blanket with a hole in the center through which the gaucho puts his head. He uses it as a coat by day and as a blanket by night. A gaucho always carries a big knife, which he uses as a sword, as a hatchet, or as a table knife. His *lariat* is a rope with weights on the ends.

Courtesy of Pan American Union

102

British Overseas Airways Corporation

Corn feeds the cattle, cattle makes meat, and meat makes money. From the skins of the cattle leather is made, and from the wool of sheep cloth is made, and from both money is made.

Argentina is so much like the United States in so many ways that it is often called the United States of South America. Both countries are alike in that they have hot weather part of the time and cold weather part of the time. But there is also a big difference between the two. Argentina has winter when the United States has summer, and Argentina has summer when the United States has winter. In Argentina, Christmas comes in the hot weather. There are snow and ice in July and August, and flowers and vegetables grow in January and February.

The seasons are caused by the amount of heat received from the sun. The earth spins on its axis as it moves around the sun. The earth does not stand straight up as it spins, but tilts on its axis. Because the earth tilts, one hemisphere is closer to the sun while the other is farther away. When the southern hemisphere is closer to the sun, it has summer because the rays of the sun are more direct. While the southern hemisphere is having summer, the northern hemisphere is having winter because it is farther away from the sun. In time the northern hemisphere comes closer to the sun and has its summer. This is why it is summer in the United States at the same time it is winter in South America.

The capital of Argentina is Buenos Aires (bway-nah-sahr' eez). The name means "Good Airs." This is the largest city in South America and is located at the mouth of the Plata River. From here cattle and grain are shipped to other countries. Beautiful buildings, subways, traffic, and parks make this city kin to all big cities in the world. The only railroad that crosses South America runs through Argentina to Chile on the west coast. Much of Argentina is flat. But to get to Chile, the railroad has to cross the Andes Mountains. Building this railroad was a great feat of engineering, and a ride on it can be an unforgettable experience.

Aerial view of Buenos Aires, Argentina

above: Close-up of mandioca, a starch-like food

Along the coast, tucked between Brazil and Argentina, is the little country of Uruguay (yoor'ah-gway). It is a country of pasturelands. Meat products are shipped from Montevideo (mahnt-ah-vah-day' o), the lively capital city at the mouth of the Plata River. It is a clean and modern city with parks and walks along the river, theaters, schools, and hospitals. A ferry boat links Montevideo with Buenos Aires.

Uruguay is considered an advanced country. Its history helps explain why. When settlers began coming to South America, Portuguese settled in Brazil. Spaniards settled everywhere else. Uruguay found itself between Spanish Argentina and Portuguese Brazil. Both Spain and Portugal wanted Uruguay and fought very hard to gain control of it. The gauchos in Uruguay had a strong spirit of independence and battled until the country became independent, too.

Bolivia (bah-live' ee-ah) and Paraguay (pair' ah-gway) are the only two countries that do not touch the sea in South America. They are landlocked countries between Brazil and Argentina.

Paraguay has been slow to develop because of transportation problems, but now river boats carry things to Argentina. Paraguay is cotton country. Other things that go down the river are tobacco and oranges. From the oranges of Paraguay an oil is taken that is used both in making perfume and for making orange flavoring. Now the government of Paraguay is working with the help of the Institute of Inter-American Affairs. They are studying the soil, and have set up a model ranch and dairy farm where they experiment with new crops, seeds, fertilizers, and machinery. Many South American countries are getting help like this. Mandioca and corn are grown as staple foods. The mandioca grows underground like a turnip. The roots are sliced and the inside is removed and made into flour and meal.

opposite top: Ramirez Beach in Montevideo, Uruguay

opposite bottom: Farmer and his bullock plow the land in Paraguay

above: A section of the city of La Paz, Bolivia

opposite: Indian poles his boat on Lake Titicaca, Bolivia

Bolivia lies within the tropics and is cut off from the Pacific by the Andes Mountains. The Andes highlands in the west have a pleasant climate. The city of La Paz, in a spectacular gorge of the La Paz River, is 12,000 feet high. Tropical lowland plains cover the eastern part of the country. Bolivia is rich in gold and silver and tin. But transportation has been difficult. Now, however, railroads carry things and roads have been built. Some of the rivers of Bolivia flow to the Amazon, but waterfalls make them impossible for shipping. The highest lake of its size in the world is Titicaca. It is more than two miles high in the mountains and is 120 miles long and 1000 feet deep. There is a port on the lake and many steamships use it. In order to get the steamships there from where they were built, they had to be taken in pieces over the mountains to the lake and put together again. The Indians of Lake Titicaca use a strange-looking boat made from reeds that grow nearby. Although Bolivia is rich in minerals, especially tin, most of the people still farm. Many of them live in houses made of mud bricks, called *adobe* and thatched with palm leaves or reeds.

Lake Titicaca is on the border between Bolivia and Peru. This lake was in the ancient kingdom of the Inca Indians. Their capital city was Cuzco, which is now in Peru. But their kingdom spread for many miles through the Andes, They did not live in huts, but in palaces. The Incas built fine roads through the mountains over which foot runners carried messages from one part of the kingdom to another. They worshipped the sun, wove beautiful cloth from the wool of the llamas and alpacas, and made many beautiful things from gold and silver. The Inca civilization flourished for hundreds of years before the Spanish came looking for gold. They found it in this Inca country and took it. They destroyed the temples to the sun in Cuzco and built Spanish churches. They covered an altar in the Cuzco cathedral with silver. Many buildings of the Spanish colonial period were destroyed by an earthquake in 1950.

One Inca city was so well hidden in the mountains that it was not discovered until 1911 by a North American archaeologist. No one knows how the granite blocks were carried up the cliff and joined to make perfect walls of buildings. It is a city of stairways, some of them carved out of solid rock. The site of this ancient city is called Machu Picchu (mah-choo peek'choo).

The Quechua (kech'ah-wah) Indians in Peru are descendents of the Incas. Most of them are farmers and they still practice the ancient customs. They raise pigs, cattle, and horses, none of which they had seen before the Spanish brought them.

Peru lies along the Pacific Ocean. Its narrow coastline is almost desert-like, but it is here that most of the people live. Three ranges of the Andes cut through the country.

Lima (lee'mah) is now the capital of Peru. After the Spaniards captured the Incas, they built this new capital city near the ocean. The city grew and kept the language and traditions that the Spaniards had brought. The Plaza de Armas, or central square, was planned by the conquerors. Facing this square are the cathedral, the arch-

Courtesy of Pan American Union

opposite: Narrow, hilly section of Cuzco, Peru

bishop's palace, the house of Pizarro, and the town hall. Pizarro was the leader of the Spanish who defeated the Incas.

Today Lima is a bustling city of about two million people. There are still many old Spanish buildings, but it is also a modern city with well-planned streets, buildings, gardens, and homes. A short drive from Lima will bring you to the beaches where the weather is pleasant almost all year.

There are some good roads in Peru and some railroads. But there are still many parts of the country that can be reached only by airplane. One of the most amazing things about the country is that ocean vessels can travel 2300 miles from the Atlantic Ocean and reach the city of Iquitos (ih-keet'ose) in Peru. They come up the Amazon River and one of its tributaries that begins in the Andes in Peru.

The Amazon River Basin in Peru is a marvelous, mysterious land of jungles. Orchids and birds and animals are found there. The modern city of Iquitos, where the steamers come, shows how man can control nature and build a city in the heart of the jungle. Many safaris and boat trips start from Iquitos.

Because of its heritage of Inca civilization, Peru is one of the most interesting South American countries to visit. In the Lima Museum of Art there are some ceremonial robes thought to be twenty-five hundred years old. There are many beautiful things from the Inca period and also many later art objects made of wood, clay, or silver.

Peru has many climates, so there are many types of natural beauty. There are snow-covered mountains with hidden villages, including Cuzco and Machu Picchu. There are lush river valleys with roaring streams. The Santa River begins high in the mountains in some beautiful lagoons and cuts its way to the west coast. The highest railroad in the world runs into the mountains of Peru. *Llamas*, animals that are something like camels without humps, still carry heavy loads through the mountains where there are no roads for trucks.

opposite top: Children pose with their llama, Peru

opposite bottom: Native woman spins wool in Peru

Ecuador (ek'wah-dore) is a little country north of Peru that straddles the equator. And the Spanish word for equator is *ecuador*. The equator, you remember, is an imaginary line that runs around the earth halfway between the North and South Poles. Lands along the equator get the most direct rays of the sun. They are usually very hot. Ecuador is not all hot because the mountains keep part of the country cool. The capital is Quito (kee'toe), more than a mile high and built in a mountain hollow. From Quito you can see two of the highest volcanoes in the world. One is quiet now and covered with snow and some glaciers. The other is still active, and fires in its crater are often reflected by clouds at night. This reflected light seems to turn the clouds pink.

The mountains of Ecuador separate the hot, humid coast on the west and the hot tropical Amazon jungles on the east.

Bananas, coffee, and rice are grown on small farms in Ecuador. But big plantations produce cocoa. Both cocoa and chocolate come from beans that grow in large pods on the *cacao* tree. The pods grow along the trunk of the tree.

Guayaquil (gwi-ah-keel') is the biggest city in Ecuador. Farm products and much balsa wood are shipped from this busy port on the Pacific. Guayaquil has a large international airport, theaters, modern hotels, apartments, and offices.

opposite: The harbor at Guayaquil, Ecuador

right: Cacao pods ready for harvest, Ecuador

below: Trimmed balsa planks ready to be floated down the Guayas River to Guayaquil for shipment

The Indians of Ecuador were a wild and savage lot.
There were headhunters who often fought with each other.
They did not fight with bows and arrows, but with huge
blowpipes as long as a man. Through these pipes they blew
clay balls or darts dipped in poison.

Many Indians still live in Ecuador. Most of them are
farmers now, but they make pottery, too, and weave cloth.
The men of the Colorado Indians, near Quito, wear a short
skirt and shoulder covering. Their hair is cut to look like a
helmet and is filled with thick red dye that makes it stand
away from the head. Both men and women paint their
bodies with red juice from a berry. This may help keep
insects from biting them. Their houses are open on the sides
and have thatched roofs.

above: Colorado Indian with blowpipe

right: Colorado Indian, Ecuador

117

Courtesy of Pan American Union

Chile is on the Pacific side of South America. It is south of Peru—a long sliver of land that runs half the length of the continent to its bleak southern tip.

The Andes Mountains separate Chile from Argentina. At one time these two countries were going to war, in spite of the wall of mountains between them. But they came to an agreement and did not fight. They melted their cannon and made a huge bronze figure of Christ holding a cross, and set it on top of a mountain. Words at the bottom of the statue say something like this: "Sooner shall these mountain crags crumble to dust than Chile and Argentina shall go to war with each other." There have been no more border fights.

The northern part of this "shoestring" republic is desert. It rains only once in several years. This country is rich in minerals. Copper is mined and sent all over the world. There is a long trough, or channel, through this land. An ancient sea once laid a wealth of nitrate here. This is used to fertilize farmlands. It is a good thing that it doesn't rain in northern Chile, for rain would dissolve the nitrate.

Fertile valleys with rich soil and a comfortable climate make up the center section of Chile.

Farther south there are forests and pasture lands, islands and inlets.

Valparaiso, or "Valley of Paradise," is an important seaport and whaling station. An earthquake in 1906 nearly destroyed the city, which now has been rebuilt. The end of an old Inca road can be seen at Valparaiso. It came 3000 miles from Quito through the mountains.

Santiago, the capital of Chile, is high in the heart of one of the fertile central valleys. Snow-capped mountains tower above this beautiful, modern city.

Copper mining town in Chile

119

The Strait of Magellan is at the southern tip of Chile. Magellan was the first man to sail around the world. He crossed the Atlantic and came to South America. He tried to get through the continent by going up the Amazon. Then he tried to get through by going up the Plata River. At last he found a narrow passageway—a strait—through the islands at the tip of Chile. He reported that he saw many fires on land at his left. Whether they were volcanoes, no longer active, or whether they were fires made by Indians, no one knows. At any rate, he called the land *Tierra del Fuego*, which means "Fireland." For hundreds of years, ships followed Magellan's route. Some of them went by open sea around the tip of the continent, called Cape Horn. But seas were rough and dangerous. Most sailors cut through the strait. A little town called Punta Arenas grew up on the strait to supply ships coming through, but its business fell off after the Panama Canal was built. Now a new business has grown up. Punta Arenas has become a shipping point for sheep grown on Tierra del Fuego.

opposite: Avenida O'Higgins, Santiago, Chile

The continent of South America is a land of ten independent nations:

> Colombia
> Venezuela
> Brazil
> Argentina
> Uruguay
> Paraguay
> Ecuador
> Chile

and three colonies of foreign nations:

> British Guiana
> Surinam (Dutch Guiana)
> French Guiana

There is great mineral wealth in the continent. There are riches in the fertile soil of the valleys and in the depth of the jungles. There is great beauty. The seas teem with life. The people in South America are learning to make better use of their treasures. The countries of South America are no longer isolated by mountains and jungles and rivers. Air transportation unites them. The future of the countries in this continent should be bright indeed.

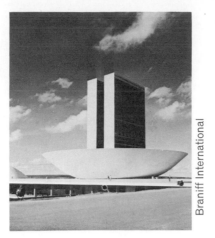

reading clockwise from above:

Senate and Chamber of Deputies Buildings in Brasilia

Palace of the Dawn in Brasilia

Peru's largest port, Callao

Loading coffee in Santos, Brazil

Surfacing a highway with asphalt, Venezuela

Highway being constructed in Venezuela

Gold mines in Peru, at 16,000 feet in the Andes Mountains

Trinidad Refinery at Ponte-a-Pierre

Power company in the Andes Mountains in Peru

Type   *Century Expanded*
Typesetter   *American Typesetting Corporation*
Printer   *The Regensteiner Corporation*